Handknit
Skirts From Tricoter

Linden Ward and Beryl Hiatt

Martingale®
& COMPANY

Handknit Skirts: From Tricoter
© 2007 by Linden Ward and Beryl Hiatt

Martingale & Company®
20205 144th Ave. NE
Woodinville, WA 98072-8478 USA
www.martingale-pub.com

Printed in China
12 11 10 09 08 07   8 7 6 5 4 3 2 1

Library of Congress Cataloging-in-Publication Data
Library of Congress Control Number: 2007028092

ISBN: 978-1-56477-835-2

CREDITS
President & CEO: Tom Wierzbicki
Publisher: Jane Hamada
Editorial Director: Mary V. Green
Managing Editor: Tina Cook
Technical Editor: Ursula Reikes
Copy Editor: Liz McGehee
Design Director: Stan Green
Assistant Design Director: Regina Girard
Illustrator: Robin Strobel
Cover Designer: Stan Green
Text Designer: Regina Girard
Photographer: Brent Kane

MISSION STATEMENT
*Dedicated to providing quality products
and service to inspire creativity.*

ACKNOWLEDGMENTS

We would like to thank two of our staff in particular: Ola and Yiming for their incredible contributions to this book. Without their counsel in the sizing, shaping, and finishing techniques, this book would not have been possible.

Thanks also to so many of our customers, whose enthusiasm, encouragement and support challenged us to keep looking for fresh ideas and new fibers for the skirts in this book.

And again, our sincere thanks to our technical editor, Ursula Reikes, and to our photographer, Brent Kane, for their professionalism and real talent in bringing our ideas into focus.

Bottom Row (left to right): Rosemarie Bonjour, Ola Sankiewicz, Dinny Brones, Beryl Hiatt, Lindy Ward, Julie Harris and Mr. Wilson (the Tricoter shop dog)

Top Row (left to right): Yiming Zhi, Tanya Parieaux, Sheila Shultz, Betsy Drahold, Marianne Francis, Teresa Marczak

CONTENTS

WHY SKIRTS?

Why a skirt book? That's the first question many of our customers asked us (only those who had not yet made their first skirt, mind you!). Well, there are a number of reasons.

- Believe it or not, skirts are *very* forgiving—almost anyone can wear knit skirts—contrary to popular belief. Very few women have what they consider to be perfect bodies, but our customers have been amazed when they put on one of our samples at how flattering it is. (We do have some secrets, but more on that later.)

- For those among us—and you know who you are—who have those "menopause moments" from time to time, skirts are a fabulous alternative to sweaters! As one of our customers said, "It's only my top half that gets hot!"

- Skirts have provided a whole new endeavor for many of our most prolific knitters. They've been noting for years, as their needles busily produce more, that they really don't *need* another sweater . . . but skirts, now there's a new frontier!

- We've tried to provide a wide array of styles and lengths. What we've found is that skirts are great at disguising our less-than-perfect attributes, but they can be equally good at emphasizing our best features. Long and sleek is perfect for those who want a more subdued look; short and sassy is great for those with fabulous legs who want to show them off.

- A number of long-term Tricoter knitters who traditionally are attracted to challenging, intricately designed sweaters have become addicted to knitting skirts as a change of pace. The rhythmic, repetitive process of knitting in the round on a project that progresses quite quickly is a welcome alternative and keeps them knitting even when they're too tired to follow a more complex pattern.

This is really a book about "thinking outside the box" when it comes to hand knitting. We have found, since we got hooked ourselves, that skirts look good on women of all ages (we've even included a toddler skirt!), in all sizes, with a broad variety of approaches to fashion, and they work with almost anything else you own. They're equally as good with knits as they are with silks, leather, even a cotton tee. They can be worn very casually or dressed up for ultimate glamour, and the choice of yarns makes them perfect for summer or winter. For the skeptics out there: *Try* knitting a skirt; you'll *love* it!

SOME SKIRT BASICS

Skirts, in general, are really quite simple to knit. There are some basics, however, that we felt important to share with you to help ensure success, both in the initial construction and in the wearing.

- The choice of fibers is critical to long-term wearability. We found that fibers need to have a fair amount of drape when knit. They should have memory (or give) on their own or should be combined with a yarn that has memory to maintain their shape and reduce inadvertent growth. The yarn or combination of yarns should be sleek enough so as not to add the look of extra pounds.

- Adding a purchased half-slip sewn into the waistband is critical to both comfort and maintaining the shape of the garment after repeated wearing. We didn't find a noticeable difference between jersey (seamless, stretchy, partially elastic or spandex fabric) slips versus cut-and-sewn (seams and less give to fabric) slips, and length is really a matter of personal choice. Slips can be similar in length to the finished skirt or noticeably shorter. The important thing is to have it as a liner.

- Because skirts are, for the most part, knit in the round, they have no defined front or back. Rotating the skirt each time it is worn further reduces the possibility of it becoming misshapen or stretched out.

- We definitely recommend the use of nonrolling elastic at least 1" wide for the waistbands—it *does* make a difference! (This is sold in most fabric stores.) Unless otherwise specified, the length of elastic for a waistband should be exactly the same as the actual waist measurement of the wearer. Once inserted into the waistband casing and sewn together, it will draw in just enough to sit comfortably at the waist.

- Our skirts are generally sized using the actual hip measurement at the widest point minus 2". This sounds dangerous; no one wants to look as if they're wearing a sausage casing, but it is really important not to have it look like a gunnysack either. Knits naturally have give, and this method of sizing has proven successful time after time—trust us! If it is fit to the widest point, it will naturally fall or drape from that point.

- Length is purely a matter of personal preference. We have found that everyone has their own preferred length, the one at which *they* feel comfortable. We have specified a length for each of our patterns that can be easily altered by lengthening or shortening the skirt in the "body portion" that is knit on the same needle for the longest time. To check your progress and determine the appropriate length for *your* skirt, slip it onto two circular needles whose combined length is greater than your hip measurement and step into it in front of a mirror. This will give you an accurate idea of how it will look. (You may want to try it with the shoes/boots you plan to wear with the skirt.)

- You may notice that we have indicated the required-stitches-per-inch gauge for each of our skirts but not the row gauge. This is because the skirts are knit to particular lengths, and the row gauge varies significantly from one needle size to the next as you knit.

GETTING STARTED

We're all eager, once the yarn has been selected and a shape determined, to get knitting— to start that project! While that does feed our need for instant gratification, more often than not, jumping into a project without swatching and measuring is often a recipe for disappointment. This is the time to make certain that you enjoy working with the yarn you have selected and that your gauge matches the pattern so you can adjust needle size if necessary.

KNITTING YOUR SWATCH

Gauge, or tension, is the most critical factor in creating garments that really fit. Most patterns are based on a specific number of stitches and rows per inch. If your knitting does not match those specifications, your finished project may not turn out as you had hoped.

To determine gauge, knit a sample swatch at least 4" wide and 4" long with the yarn and needles you will use for your project. Because the stitches at the end of the knitting tend to be somewhat distorted, you'll want to measure at least one stitch in from the selvage edges of the swatch. Therefore, cast on at least two more stitches than needed to make 4" of knitting width. Work the pattern stitch specified to check the gauge; if no pattern is given, work the swatch in stockinette stitch. If the pattern is complex (color work or lace), work a larger swatch, perhaps 6" to 8" square.

To measure the swatch, lay it flat. Place a tape measure parallel to a row of stitches and count the number of stitches (including fractions of inches) that make 4". Divide the number of stitches in the 4" swatch by 4 to get the number of stitches per inch. This is your gauge.

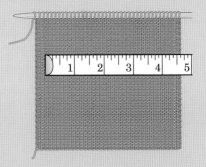

Compare the gauge to that specified in your pattern. If your swatch has too few stitches, your work is too loose; try again with smaller needles. If your swatch has too many stitches, your work is too tight; try larger needles or a different yarn. You are ready to begin knitting when your gauge matches that specified by the pattern.

Periodically as you knit, lay your work flat. Without stretching it, measure every few inches to see if your gauge has changed. Continue to measure both the length and width of your piece as you knit. It is not uncommon for your gauge to change significantly due to increased stress, fatigue, or lack of concentration. It is relatively simple to adjust your pattern, increasing or decreasing a couple of stitches at this point. This is a habit that you should continue to practice throughout all of your knitting.

SUBSTITUTING YARNS

If you're interested in using a yarn other than one specified, remember to select a yarn or combination of yarns that knits to the same gauge. This can only be determined by swatching. Refer to "Yarn Information" on page 77 for yarn amounts so that you can gauge appropriate substitutes and quantities. You may need to adjust needle size to get the gauge. Don't be afraid to experiment with your swatch to make certain that you are happy with the look and feel of the swatch before you proceed.

~ 9

ADRIENNE

A great customer of ours was looking for a terrific
holiday skirt in black, but something she wouldn't
see at every party. Ola helped her with this design,
and it's gotten many compliments.

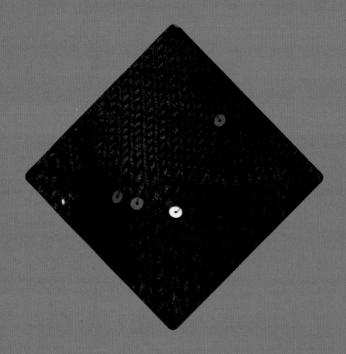

SIZES

Extra Small
(Small, Medium, Large, Extra Large)

Actual Hip Measurement:
32 (36, 40, 44, 50)"

Finished Hip Measurement:
30 (34, 38, 42, 48)"

Finished Length: 23"*

*Finished length is measured from bottom
of waistband. Length of skirt can be altered
as desired by lengthening or shortening skirt
in section worked on size 6 needle.

MATERIALS

A 5 (6, 6, 7, 8) skeins of Baby Cashmerino from Debbie Bliss, color 340300 (black)

B 1 (1, 1, 1, 2) skeins of Lazer FX from Berroco, color 6008 (black)

US 11, 6, and 5 circular needles, all 24" to 26" long, or size to obtain gauge

Stitch marker

1"-wide nonrolling elastic cut to same length as actual waist measurement

Size H-8 (5 mm) crochet hook

Ready-made half-slip at least 3" shorter than finished length of skirt

GAUGE

A yarn or combination of yarns that, when held tog as one, knits to 21.5 sts over 4" in St st on size 6 needle

DIRECTIONS

- With size 11 needle and 1 strand of A, CO 162 (184, 206, 238, 260) sts. Join into rnd, taking care not to twist sts; pm, and knit every rnd.

- On 4th and every following 8th rnd, knit 1 rnd with 1 strand of B held tog with 1 strand of A.

- At 6" from bottom, switch to size 6 needle and knit every rnd.

- At 18½" from bottom, switch to size 5 needle and knit every rnd.

- At 23" from bottom, work in K1, P1 ribbing for 2½".

- BO all sts in patt.

FINISHING

- Fold 1¼" of waistband over to inside of skirt; blindstitch in place. Insert elastic band and sew ends tog.

- Using crochet hook, finish hemline with 1 row of sc using 2 strands of A held tog.

- Block and steam skirt to desired measurements.

- Attach waistband of ready-made half-slip to bottom inside edge of waistband.

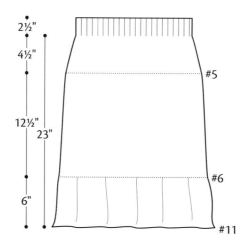

BELLA

We loved the idea of incorporating beading
in a skirt, and this hemline treatment
creates the gentle flared silhouette
with the beads themselves.

SIZES

Extra Small
(Small, Medium, Large)

Actual Hip Measurement:
34 (36, 38, 40)"

Finished Hip Measurement:
32 (34, 36, 38)"

Finished Length: 21"*

*Finished length is measured from bottom
of waistband. Length of skirt can be altered
as desired by lengthening or shortening skirt
in section worked on size 6 needle.*

MATERIALS

2 (2, 2, 3) skeins of Rayon Metallic from Blue Heron Yarns, color Deep Old Gold

3 skeins of Kidsilk Night from Rowan, color 614 Macbeth

1800 size 6 mm seed beads, color metallic purple/green

Size 6 and 4 circular needles, both 24" to 26" long, or size to obtain gauge

1"-wide nonrolling elastic cut to same length as actual waist measurement

Tapestry needle and sewing thread

Stitch marker

Ready-made half-slip at least 3" shorter than finished length of skirt

GAUGE

A yarn or combination of yarns that, when held tog as one, knits to 21.5 sts over 4" in St st on size 6 needle

DIRECTIONS

B7, B6, B5, etc.: Slide number of beads indicated down yarn to needle before cont to knit or purl next set of sts. Slide same number of beads on WS as you did on RS.

- Thread tapestry needle with a length of sewing thread approx 8" long. Secure ends of thread with a knot; thread 1 strand each of Rayon Metallic and Kidsilk Night through loop created with thread and string 500 beads onto yarn. You are now ready to CO.

- With size 6 needle and 1 strand each of Rayon Metallic and Kidsilk Night held tog, *CO 21 (22, 24, 25) sts, B7, rep from * 8 times, end K1—169 (177, 193, 201) total sts and 56 beads.

- Working back and forth in St st (*not* in rnd until beading is completed), purl or knit 21 (22, 24, 25), B7 as established on next 7 rows. Work rem bead rows by working more knit or purl sts as required and less beads in every 8-row rep:

Work 8 rows with B6 rather than B7.

Work 8 rows with B5 rather than B6.

Work 8 rows with B4 rather than B5.

Work 8 rows with B3 rather than B4.

Work 8 rows with B2 rather than B3.

Work 8 rows with B1 rather than B2.

As you run out of beads, cut yarn at beg or end of row only, and thread another 500 beads to cont. When 8th row of last 8-row rep with 1 bead at each beaded section is complete, join into rnd (knit first and last st of row tog and pm). This completes beading for skirt—168 (176, 192, 200) sts rem. Cont on size 6 needles, and knit every rnd.

- At 14½" from bottom, switch to size 4 needle, knit every rnd, and dec 8 sts evenly across rnd every 10th rnd 5 times—128 (136, 152, 160) sts.

- At 21" from bottom, work K1, P1 ribbing for 1½".

- BO all sts in patt.

FINISHING

- Finish waistband using Style C (see page 76).

- Sew seam on bottom portion of skirt where it was knit back and forth.

- Block and steam skirt to desired measurements.

- Attach waistband of ready-made half-slip to bottom inside edge of waistband.

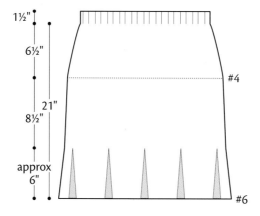

CASSANDRA

Beryl has always loved pulling together a basket of favorite yarns and then just swatching at random until pleased with the overall look. By concentrating the most heavily textured fibers at the bottom, she created a dramatic border, and the body of the skirt is slim and flattering.

SIZES

Extra Small
(Small, Medium, Large, Extra Large)

Actual Hip Measurement:
32 (34, 36, 38, 40)"

Finished Hip Measurement:
30 (32, 34, 36, 38)"

Finished Length: 32"*

*Finished length is measured from bottom of waistband. Length of skirt can be altered as desired by lengthening or shortening skirt in section worked on size 10 needle.

MATERIALS

A 2 (3, 3, 3, 4) skeins of Dream from Tahki, color 015 (black)

B 4 (5, 5, 6, 6) skeins of Cashmerino Astrakhan from Debbie Bliss, color 31001 (black)

C 1 (1, 1, 2, 2) skeins of Boise from Karabella, color 58 (black)

D 2 (3, 3, 4, 4) skeins of Poly Moire Eyelash from Habu Textiles, color 7 (black)

E 1 (2, 2, 2, 2) skeins of Tobi Moire from Habu Textiles, color 90 (black)

F 1 (1, 1, 1, 2) skeins of Cleo from Muench, color 381131 (black)

G 1 skein of Wool Cotton from Rowan Yarns, color 908 (black)

US 15, 10, 8, and 6 circular needles, all 24" to 26" long, or size to obtain gauge

Stitch marker

1"-wide nonrolling elastic cut to same length as actual waist measurement

Ready-made half-slip at least 3" shorter than finished length of skirt

GAUGE

A yarn or combination of yarns that, when held tog as one, knits to 14 sts over 4" in St st on size 10 needle

HEMLINE STRIPING PATTERN

Knit 3 rnds with 1 strand each of D and C held tog.

Knit 2 rnds with 1 strand each of F and A held tog.

Knit 6 rnds with 1 strand each of E, C, and A held tog.

Knit 2 rnds with 1 strand each of F and A held tog.

Knit 4 rnds with 1 strand each of D and C held tog.

Knit 2 rnds with 1 strand each of F and A held tog.

Knit 8 rnds with 1 strand each of E, C, and A held tog.

Knit 5 rnds with 1 strand each of F and A held tog.

Knit 4 rnds with 1 strand each of D and C held tog.

Hemline striping patt is worked only once.

SKIRT STRIPING PATTERN

Knit 4" with 1 strand each of B and A held tog.

Knit 2 rnds with 1 strand each of F and A held tog.

Rep knit 4" and 2 rnds as indicated for striping patt.

DIRECTIONS

- With size 15 needle and 1 strand each of D and C held tog, CO 123 (130, 136, 144, 151) sts. Join into rnd, taking care not to twist sts; pm and work hemline striping patt.

- At 11" from bottom, switch to size 10 needle and dec 17 (18, 18, 18, 17) sts evenly across rnd—106 (112,118, 126, 134) sts. Work skirt striping pattern.

- At 30" from bottom, switch to size 8 needle and cont for 2" with skirt striping patt.

- At 32" from bottom, switch to size 6 needle, and with 1 strand each of A and G held tog, work 3" in K1, P1 ribbing.

- BO all sts in patt.

FINISHING

- Fold 1½" of waistband over to inside of skirt; blindstitch in place. Insert elastic band and sew ends tog.

- Block and steam skirt to desired measurements.

- Attach waistband of ready-made half-slip to bottom inside edge of waistband.

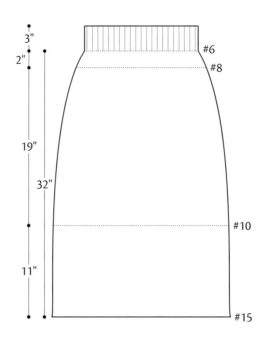

3"

2"

#6

#8

19"

32"

#10

11"

#15

DYLAN

Julie loved the look of strong color transitions with a unifying strand of a neutral, spaced-dyed fiber to tie them all together. This "faux button front" skirt gives the look of a skirt with front closure but is actually knit most of the way in the round.

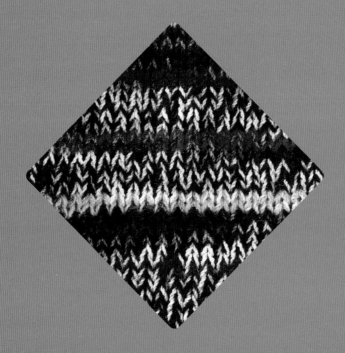

SIZES

Extra Small
(Small, Medium, Large)

Actual Hip Measurement:
34 (36, 38, 40)"

Finished Hip Measurement:
32 (34, 36, 38)"

Finished Length: 28"*

Finished length is measured from bottom of waistband. Length of skirt can be altered as desired by lengthening or shortening skirt in section worked on size 6 needle.

MATERIALS

A 4 skeins of Dream Print from Tahki, color 060

Cashmere 7000 from Filatura di Crosa/ TSC Inc. in the following amounts and colors:

B 1 skein of color 400002 Black

C 1 skein of color 301913 Chartreuse

D 1 skein of color 712014 Teal

E 1 skein of color 400003 Cranberry

US 7, 6, and 5 circular needles, all 24" to 26" long, or size to obtain gauge

8 stitch markers

5 buttons, approximately ⅜" diameter

1"-wide nonrolling elastic cut to same length as actual waist measurement

Ready-made half-slip at least 9" shorter than finished length of skirt

GAUGE

A yarn or combination of yarns that, when held tog as one, knits to 21 sts over 4" in St st on size 6 needle

STRIPING PATTERN

4 rows with 1 strand each of B and A held tog

2 rows with 1 strand each of E and A held tog

4 rows with 1 strand each of B and A held tog

2 rows with 1 strand each of C and A held tog

4 rows with 1 strand each of B and A held tog

2 rows with 1 strand each of D and A held tog

Rep these 18 rows for striping patt.

DIRECTIONS

- With size 7 needle and 1 strand each of B and A held tog, CO 226 (236, 246, 256) sts. Working in striping patt back and forth in St st, on next row, K15 (20, 18, 23), pm, [K28 (28, 30, 30), pm] 7 times, K15 (20, 18, 23). Dec 1 st *after* first 4 markers and *before* last 4 markers every 8th row 7 times; use different-colored marker for beg of rnd. Number of sts at beg and end of row will rem constant while number of sts between markers will dec until 170 (180, 190, 200) total sts rem. Cont in striping patt, working back and forth.

- At 9" from bottom, switch to size 6 needle, remove markers except for beg of row marker. Join work into rnd, cont in striping patt, knit every rnd.

- At 23" from bottom, dec 8 sts evenly in rnd—162 (172, 182, 192) sts. Cont in striping patt, knit every rnd.

- At 25" from bottom, dec 8 sts evenly in rnd—154 (164, 174, 184) sts. Cont in striping patt, knit every rnd.

- At 28" from bottom, switch to size 5 needle and with 1 strand each of B and A held tog, work in K1, P1 ribbing for 1½".

- BO all sts in patt.

FINISHING

- With size 5 needle and 2 strands of B held tog, PU 48 sts on RS (left side as you face work) of front skirt opening and work in K1, P1 ribbing for ¾", placing 5 buttonholes, evenly spaced, in 3rd row. For buttonhole, work YO, K2tog for each buttonhole.

- Rep PU on opposite side of opening and work in K1, P1 ribbing for ¾". Sew on buttons to correspond with buttonholes on opposite band.

- Finish waistband using Style C (see page 76).

- Block and steam skirt to desired measurements.

- Attach waistband of ready-made half-slip to bottom inside edge of waistband.

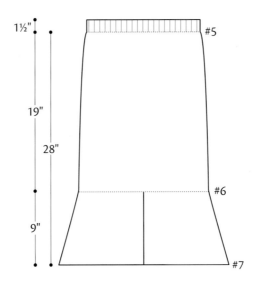

1½" #5
19"
28"
9" #6
#7

ELAINE

A touch of black net peeking out at the hemline
and the delicate row of mother-of-pearl
buttons with seed-beading trim give
this skirt lots of personality.

MATERIALS

A 3 (4, 4, 5) skeins of Diasantafe from Diakeito, color 530 Gray Multi

B 3 (4, 4, 5) skeins of Opal Lamé from Berroco, color 0203 Silver Multi

C 1 skein of Victoria from S. Charles Collezione, color 12 Black

16 (18, 20, 22) mother-of-pearl buttons, ½" to ¾" diameter

16 (18, 20, 22) silver seed beads

1 yard of black nylon or polyester tulle

US 8 and 7 circular needles, both 24" to 26" long, or size to obtain gauge

8 stitch markers

1"-wide nonrolling elastic cut to same length as actual waist measurement

Size D-3 (3.25 mm) crochet hook

Ready-made half-slip at least 2" shorter than finished length of skirt

GAUGE

A yarn or combination of yarns that, when held tog as one, knits to 19 sts over 4" in St st on size 7 needle

DIRECTIONS

- With size 8 needle and 1 strand each of A and B held tog, CO 192 (202, 212, 222) sts. Join into rnd, taking care not to twist sts; knit and place 8 markers 24 (25, 26, 27) sts apart; use a different-color marker for beg of rnd. Note that you will have 24 (27, 30, 33) sts between 7th and 8th markers.

- Knit every rnd, dec 1 st before each marker every 9th rnd 5 times—152 (162, 172, 182) sts.

- At 6½" from bottom, switch to size 7 needles and 1 strand of C, knit every rnd for 1".

- At 7½" from bottom, cut C and switch back to 1 strand each of A and B held tog, knit every rnd.

- At 15½" from bottom, remove existing markers and insert 6 markers placed every 25 (27, 28, 30) sts. Note that you will have 27 (27, 32, 32) sts between 5th and 6th markers. Knit every rnd, dec before each marker every 10th rnd 4 times—128 (138, 148, 158) sts.

- At 20½" from bottom, work K1, P1 ribbing for 1½".

- BO all sts in patt.

FINISHING

- Finish waistband using Style C (see page 76).

- Place buttons approx 1" apart, centered on black band, and sew in place, securing a silver seed bead in center of each button.

- Using crochet hook and 1 strand of A, work 1 row of sc at hemline.

- From yard of tulle, cut 2 strips, 9" x 36". Sew 2 strips tog at 9" ends to make a large circle. Using black thread and working about ½" from top edge, gather tube to match inside diameter of skirt at black contrast band. Pin in place on inside of skirt so that approx 1" of tulle extends below hemline, blindstitch in place. Note that there is no hem on tulle at bottom of skirt; cut edge is finished look.

- Block and steam skirt to desired measurements.

- Attach waistband of ready-made half-slip to bottom inside edge of waistband.

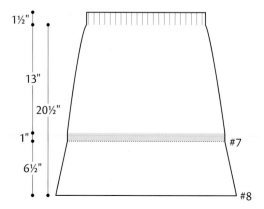

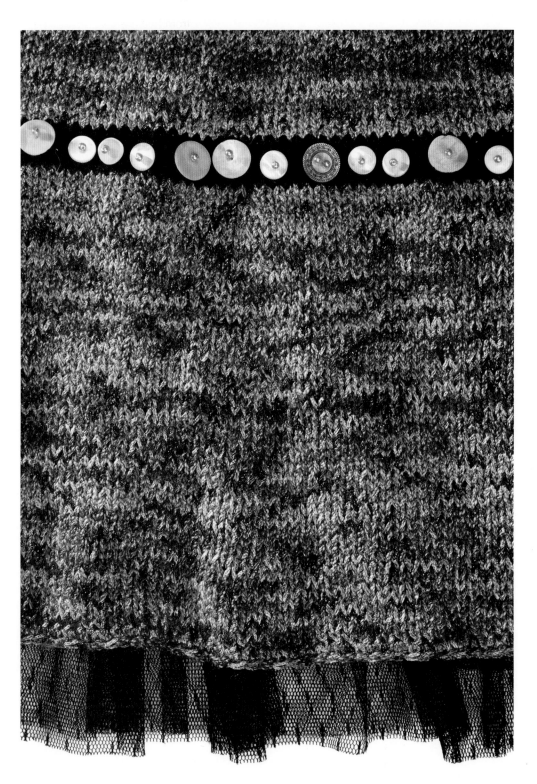

FELICITY

The half-linen stitch used throughout this skirt gives it body and helps maintain its shape. Changing needle sizes as you knit creates the subtle shaping. We loved the combination of luxury fibers in this very sophisticated slim skirt.

SIZES

Extra Small
(Small, Medium, Large)

Actual Hip Measurement:
33 (35, 37, 39)"

Finished Hip Measurement:
31 (33, 35, 37)"

Finished Length: 19½"*

*Finished length for this skirt includes waistband portion of skirt. Length of skirt can be altered as desired by lengthening or shortening skirt in section worked on size 7 needle.

MATERIALS

A 4 (5, 5, 6) skeins of Cashmere 100 from Filatura di Crosa, color 200571 Brown

B 3 (3, 4, 4) skeins of Gioiello from Filatura di Crosa, color 18 Golden Brown

US 4, 5, 6, and 7 circular needles, all 24" to 26" long, or size to obtain gauge

Stitch marker

1"-wide nonrolling elastic cut to same length as actual waist measurement

Size E-4 (3.5 mm) crochet hook

Ready-made half-slip at least 2" shorter than finished length of skirt

GAUGE

A yarn or combination of yarns that, when held tog as one, knits to 19.5 sts over 4" in half linen st on size 7 needles

HALF LINEN STITCH (WORKED IN THE ROUND)

Rnd 1: Knit.

Rnd 2: *K1, sl 1 wyif, rep from *.

Rnd 3: Knit.

Rnd 4: *Sl 1 wyif, K1, rep from *.

Rep rnds 1–4.

DIRECTIONS

- With size 4 needle and 1 strand each of A and B held tog, CO 152 (162, 172, 182) sts using Chinese cast on (see page 74). Join into rnd, taking care not to twist sts; pm and work in half linen st.

- At 6" from beg, switch to size 7 needle and cont in half linen st.

- At 12½" from beg, switch to size 6 needle and cont in half linen st.

- At 16" from beg, switch to size 5 needle and cont in half linen st.

- At 17½" from beg, switch to size 4 needle and cont in half linen st.

- At 19½" from beg, BO all sts.

FINISHING

- Using crochet hook and 1 strand each of A and B held tog, work 1 row of sc around BO edge at waist.

- Finish waistband using Style C (see page 76).

- Block and steam skirt to desired measurements.

- Attach waistband of ready-made half-slip to bottom inside edge of waistband.

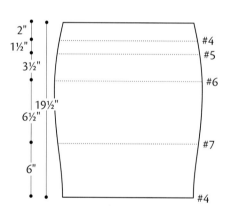

GABRIELLE

The use of a great sturdy sock yarn held together with a soft kid mohair to blend the colors opened up a brand new world for us. What a great alternative use for sock yarn! The introduction of a cashmere and merino blend for the color work adds softness, rich color, and contrast.

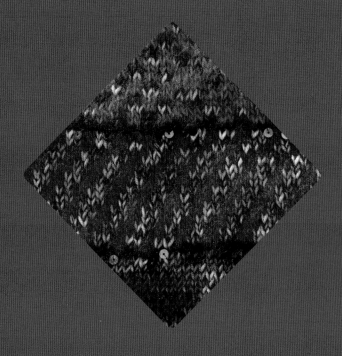

SIZES

Small
(Medium, Large, Extra Large)

Actual Hip Measurement:
34 (38, 42, 48)"

Finished Hip Measurement:
32 (36, 40, 46)"

Finished Length: 27"*

Finished length is measured from bottom of waistband. Length of skirt can be altered as desired by lengthening or shortening skirt in striped section after color-work band and before shaping.

MATERIALS

Socks that Rock from Blue Moon Fiber Arts in the following amounts and colors:

MC 2 (2, 3, 3) skeins of color Farmhouse

CCA 1 skein of color Alina

CCB 1 skein of color Christmas Rock

A 3 (3, 4, 4) skeins of Baby Kid Extra from Filatura di Crosa, color 326 Black

Boise from Karabella in the following amounts and colors:

B 1 skein of color 58 Black

C 1 skein of color 63 Red

D 1 skein of color 61 Olive

E 1 skein of color 62 Rust

F 1 skein of Lazer FX from Berroco, color 6008 Black

US 6 and 7 circular needles, 24" to 26" long, or size to obtain gauge

9 stitch markers

1"-wide nonrolling elastic cut to same length as actual waist measurement

GAUGE

A yarn or combination of yarns that, when held tog as one, knits to 20 sts over 4" in St st on size 7 needle

COLOR-WORK BAND

Diagonal pattern is worked with 2 sts in one yarn combination and 2 sts in another yarn. On EOR, colors are moved 1 st to right or left as indicated.

Knit 1 rnd with 1 strand each of B and F held tog.

Knit 16 rnds, alternating 2 sts of 1 strand each of CCA and A held tog and 2 sts of C, moving diagonal 1 st to *right* on EOR.

Knit 1 rnd with 1 strand each of B and F held tog.

Knit 16 rnds, alternating 2 sts of 1 strand each of MC and A held tog and 2 sts of D, switching checkered patt on EOR.

Knit 1 rnd with 1 strand each of B and F held tog.

Knit 16 rnds, alternating 2 sts of 1 strand each of CCB and A held tog and 2 sts of E, moving diagonal 1 st to *left* on EOR.

Knit 1 rnd with 1 strand each of B and F held tog.

This color-work band is worked only once.

STRIPING SEQUENCE

Knit 4 rnds with 1 strand each of MC and A held tog.

Knit 4 rnds with 1 strand each of CCA and A held tog.

Knit 4 rnds with 1 strand each of MC and A held tog.

Knit 4 rnds with 1 strand each of CCB and A held tog.

Rep 16-rnd sequence as needed to end of waistband.

DIRECTIONS

- With size 7 needle and 1 strand each of MC and A held tog, CO 196 (220, 256, 276) sts. Join rnd, pm; use different-colored marker for beg of rnd.

- **Next rnd:** K25 (28, 32, 35), pm, [K49 (55, 64, 69), pm] 3 times, end K24 (27, 32, 34).

- Cont in St st and working in striping sequence, dec 1 st after each marker (except beg of rnd marker) every 3" for a total of 2 times—188 (212, 248, 268) sts.

- At 7" from bottom, work 8" of color-work band. On last rnd of color-work band, dec 28 (32, 38, 38) sts evenly across rnd—160 (180, 210, 230) sts.

- Beg striping sequence on next rnd and cont for balance of skirt.

- At 21" from bottom, add 4 markers evenly spaced between existing markers (do *not* count beg of rnd marker)—8 dec markers. Dec 1 st after each marker every 8 rnds 5 times—120 (140, 170, 190) sts.

- At 27" from bottom, switch to size 6 needle and work in K1, P1 ribbing for 2½".

- BO all sts in patt.

FINISHING

- Fold 1¼" of waistband over to inside of skirt; blindstitch in place. Insert elastic band and sew ends tog.

- Block and steam skirt to desired measurements.

- Attach waistband of ready-made half-slip to bottom inside edge of waistband.

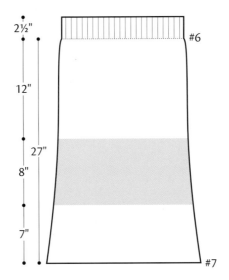

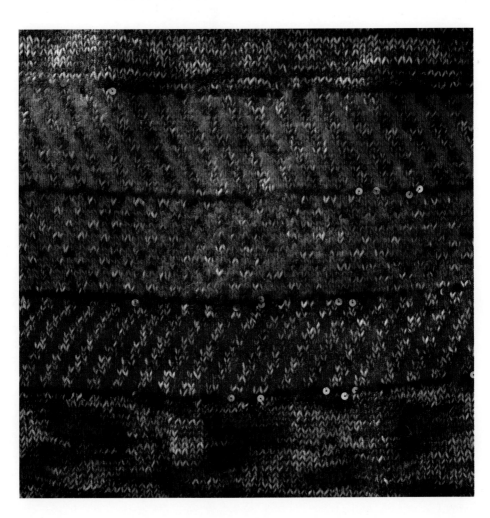

HANNAH

We discovered the Diakeito line of fibers at a trade show several
seasons ago. We loved the complex colorways and soft, drapey
texture of the knitted yarns. The combination of two very different
yarns and colors blends beautifully in this all-season skirt.

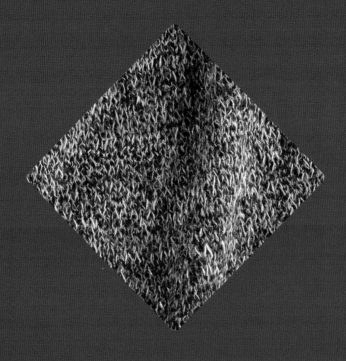

SIZES

Extra Small
(Small, Medium, Large, Extra Large)

Actual Hip Measurement:
32 (36, 40, 44, 50)"

Finished Hip Measurement:
30 (34, 38, 42, 48)"

Finished Length: 27"*

*Finished length is measured from bottom of
waistband. Length of skirt can be altered as
desired by lengthening or shortening skirt
in section worked on size 8 needle.*

MATERIALS

A 5 (5, 5, 6, 6) skeins of Dialent from Diakeito, color 708 Black/Silver

B 5 (5, 5, 6, 6) skeins of Diacosta from Diakeito, color 228 Black Multi

C 1 skein of Cork Chenille from Habu Textiles, color 12 Charcoal

US 13, 8, 7, and 6 circular needles, all 24" to 26" long, or size to obtain gauge

Stitch marker

1"-wide nonrolling elastic cut to same length as actual waist measurement

Size H-8 (5 mm) crochet hook

Ready-made half-slip at least 3" shorter than finished length of skirt

GAUGE

A yarn or combination of yarns that, when held tog as one, knits to 19.5 sts over 4" in St st on size 8 needle

DIRECTIONS

- With size 13 needle and 1 strand each of A, B, and C held tog, CO 146 (165, 184, 204, 233) sts; join into rnd, taking care not to twist sts; pm and knit every rnd.

- At 3" from bottom, cut C, switch to size 8 needle, and knit every rnd.

- At 21" from bottom, switch to size 7 needle, and knit every rnd.

- At 24" from bottom, switch to size 6 needle, and knit every rnd.

- At 27" from bottom, work in K1, P1 ribbing for 2½".

- BO all sts in patt.

FINISHING

- Fold 1¼" of waistband over to inside of skirt; blindstitch in place. Insert elastic band and sew ends tog.

- Using crochet hook, finish hemline with 1 row of sc using 1 strand each of all 3 yarns.

- Block and steam skirt to desired measurements.

- Attach waistband of ready-made half-slip to bottom inside edge of waistband.

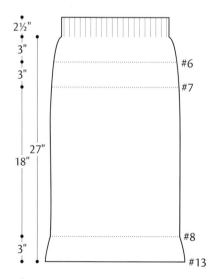

ILSA

The Diasantafe is a beautiful fiber all by itself, but we thought it needed to be toned down a bit for a skirt. The black Soft Kid was a perfect choice to blend the colors and add the bit of black that ties it to almost anything in your closet.

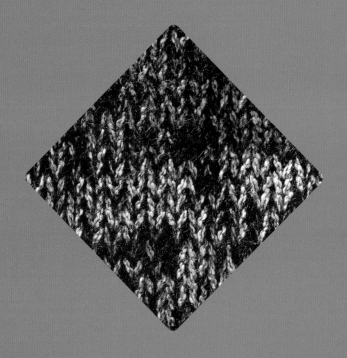

SIZES

Extra Small
(Small, Medium, Large, Extra Large)

Actual Hip Measurement:
35 (37, 39, 41, 45)"

Finished Hip Measurement:
33 (35, 37, 39, 43)"

Finished Length: 34"*

Finished length is measured from bottom of waistband. Length of skirt can be altered as desired by lengthening or shortening skirt in section worked on size 9 needle.

MATERIALS

A 6 (6, 7, 7, 7) skeins of Diasantafe from Diakeito, color 513 Pink Multi

B 6 (6, 7, 7, 7) skeins of Soft Kid from GGH, color 27 Black

1"-wide elastic cut to same length as actual waist measurement

US 9 and 7 circular needles, both 24" to 26" long, or size to obtain gauge

8 stitch markers

Size G-6 (4.0 mm) crochet hook

GAUGE

A yarn or combination of yarns that, when held tog as one, knits to 16.5 sts over 4" in St st on size 9 needle

DIRECTIONS

- With size 9 needle and 1 strand each of A and B held tog, CO 164 (172, 180,188, 204)) sts. Join into rnd, taking care not to twist sts; pm and knit 1 rnd. On next rnd, knit around and pm after 41 (43, 45, 47, 51) sts 3 times; use a different-color marker for beg of rnd.

- Knit every rnd and dec 1 st after each marker every 12 rnds 7 times—136 (144, 152, 160, 176) sts. Cont without dec.

- At 28" from bottom, add 4 more markers evenly spaced between the 4 existing markers—8 markers with 17 (18, 19, 20, 22) sts between markers.

- Knit every rnd and dec 1 st after each marker every 12 rnds 4 times—104 (112, 120, 128, 144) sts. Cont without dec.

- At 34" from bottom, switch to size 7 needle and work in K1, P1 ribbing for 2½".

- BO all sts in patt.

FINISHING

- Fold 1¼" of waistband over to inside of skirt; blindstitch in place. Insert elastic band and sew ends tog.

- Using crochet hook and 1 strand of B, work 1 row of sc at hemline, adjusting sts as needed to end with total sts divisible by 3, do not turn. **Next rnd:** *Ch 5, sk 2 sc, sc in next st, rep from * around, sl st in base of first ch-5, do not turn. **Next rnd:** Ch 3, *sc in ch-5 space, ch 5, rep from * around, ending with sl st in last ch-5 sp.

- Block and steam skirt to desired measurements.

- Attach waistband of ready-made half-slip to bottom inside edge of waistband.

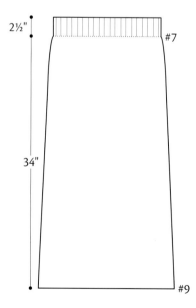

JANELLE

We wanted a tweedy skirt with a bit of movement. The use of short rows works great to create the silhouette, while the combination of a skinny bouclé and a hand-dyed cashmere create the tweedy appearance.

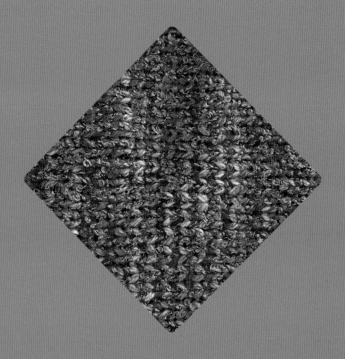

SIZES

Extra Small
(Small, Medium, Large)

Actual Hip Measurement:
33 (37, 40, 44)"

Finished Hip Measurement:
31 (35, 38, 42)"

Finished Length: 23"*

Finished length is measured from bottom of waistband. Length of skirt can be altered as desired by lengthening or shortening skirt in section worked on size 8 needle.

MATERIALS

A 2 (2, 2, 3) skeins of Silk/Cashmere from Jade Sapphire, color 40 Cashouflage

B 4 (4, 4, 5) skeins of Stained Glass from Ironstone Yarns, color 9 Caramel

Small amount of waste yarn for cast on

US 8 straight or circular needles or size to obtain gauge

US 5 circular needle, 24" to 26" long

1"-wide nonrolling elastic cut to same length as actual waist measurement

Ready-made half-slip at least 2" shorter than finished length of skirt

GAUGE

A yarn or combination of yarns that, when held tog as one, knits to 14.5 sts and 27 rows over 4" in St st on size 8 needles

NOTE: Because this skirt is knit from side to side, the row gauge is as important as the stitch gauge on this project. Swatching is very important to ensure a proper fit!

SHORT-ROW FLARES

Wrap next st: bring yarn forward between needle tips, sl next st on left needle to right needle, move yarn back between needle tips.

To create each of the flares in this skirt, after working the specified number of complete rows, beg short rows on RS of work as follows:

Row 1: K32, wrap next st. Turn.

Row 2: Purl back.

Rows 3–12: Rep rows 1 and 2 with 31 sts, 30 sts, 29 sts, 28 sts, and 27 sts.

Row 13: *Knit across, knitting each wrap tog with st—82 sts.

Row 14: Purl back.

Beg second side of flare:

Row 15: K27, wrap next st. Turn.

Row 16: Purl back.

Row 17: K28, remembering to knit each wrap tog with st, wrap next st. Turn.

Row 18: Purl back.

Rows 19–26: Rep rows 17 and 18 with 29 sts, 30 sts, 31 sts, and 32 sts.

DIRECTIONS

Skirt is worked from side to side.

- With size 8 needle and waste yarn, CO 82 sts. On next (WS) row, switch to 2 strands of A and 1 strand of B held tog. Work 14 (16, 18, 20) rows in St st, then work first 26-row flare.

- *Work 28 (32, 34, 38) rows in St st over all sts, then work 26-row flare, rep from * 5 more times.

- Work 14 (16, 18, 20) rows in St st, then remove waist yarn from CO row and graft sts tog with last knitted row to create skirt.

FINISHING

- With size 5 needle and 2 strands of A and 1 of B held tog, PU 110 (126, 140, 154) sts from top edge of skirt and work 1¼" in K1, P1 ribbing. BO in patt.

- Finish waistband using Style C (see page 76).

- Steam flares to open them up and keep hemline flat.

- Attach waistband of ready-made half-slip to bottom inside edge of waistband.

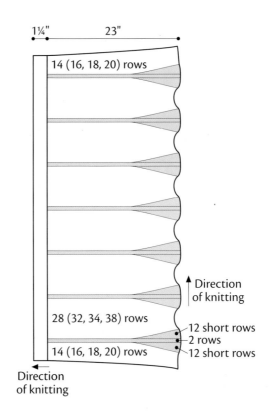

1¼"   23"

14 (16, 18, 20) rows

Direction
of knitting

28 (32, 34, 38) rows

12 short rows
2 rows
12 short rows

14 (16, 18, 20) rows

← Direction
of knitting

MATERIALS

A 1 (2, 4) skeins of Big Wool Fusion from Rowan, color 02 Soft Chartreuse

B 1 skein of Glowlash from Erdal, color 27 Chartreuse

US 11 and 13 circular needles, both 24" to 26" long, or size to obtain gauge

Size H-8 (5 mm) crochet hook

Stitch marker

GAUGE

A yarn or combination of yarns that, when held tog as one, knits to 8.5 sts over 4" in St st on size 13 needles

DIRECTIONS

- With size 11 needle and 1 strand each of A and B held tog, CO 141 (171, 222) sts. Join into rnd, taking care not to twist sts; pm and work first 5 rounds as follows:

Rnd 1: Knit.

Rnd 2: Purl.

Rnd 3: *K1, K2tog, rep from * around— 94 (114, 148) sts.

Rnd 4: Purl.

Rnd 5: K2tog around—47 (57, 74) sts.

- On next rnd, switch to size 13 needle and 1 strand of A, cont in garter st (purl 1 rnd, knit 1 rnd).

- At 7 (10, 12)" from bottom, switch to size 11 needle, dec 1 (1, 0) st in next rnd—46 (56, 74) sts. Work in K1, P1 ribbing for 2".

- BO all sts in patt.

FINISHING

- Make a twisted cord (see page 75) approx 40 (50, 60)" long using 1 strand of A. Use crochet hook to pull cord through ribbed waistband.

- Block and steam skirt to desired measurements.

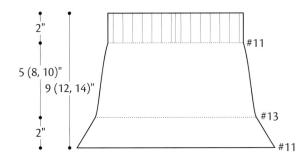

LIANNE

Mixing a textured cottonlike blend and a skinny wool/nylon blend gives this skirt the perfect all-season combination of colors and textures with enough stability to keep its shape. Never be afraid to mix unusual colors— they often create the most interesting results.

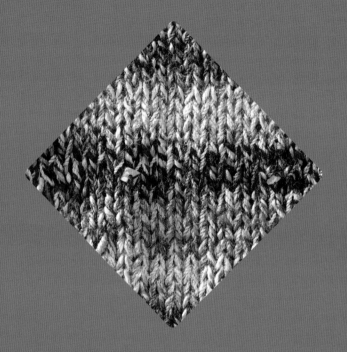

SIZES

Extra Small
(Small, Medium, Large, Extra Large)

Actual Hip Measurement:
32 (36, 40, 44, 50)"

Finished Hip Measurement:
30 (34, 38, 42, 48)"

Finished Length: 26"*

Finished length is measured from bottom of waistband. Length of skirt can be altered as desired by lengthening or shortening skirt in section worked on size 10 needle.

MATERIALS

A 5 (5, 5, 6, 6) skeins of Sakura from Noro, color 2 Blue Multi

B 3 (3, 3, 4, 4) skeins of Dream from Tahki, color 063 Blue Multi

C 1 skein of Shingle from Louisa Harding, color Black

US 15, 10, 9, 8, and 7 circular needles, all 24" to 26" long, or size to obtain gauge

Stitch marker

1"-wide nonrolling elastic cut to same length as actual waist measurement

Size H-8 (5 mm) crochet hook

Ready-made half-slip at least 3" shorter than finished length of skirt

GAUGE

A yarn or combination of yarns that, when held tog as one, knits to 16.75 sts over 4" in St st on size 10 needle

DIRECTIONS

- With size 15 needle and 1 strand each of A and B held tog, CO 126 (144,160, 176, 202) sts. Join into rnd, taking care not to twist sts; pm and knit every rnd.

- Approx every 3", add 1 strand of C to A and B and knit 1 rnd only. Cont to knit every rnd.

- At 6" from bottom, switch to size 10 needle and knit every rnd.

- At 20" from bottom, switch to size 9 needle and knit every rnd.

- At 23" from bottom, switch to size 8 needle and knit every rnd.

- At 26" from bottom, switch to size 7 needle and work in K1, P1 ribbing for 2½".

- BO all sts.

FINISHING

- Fold 1¼" of waistband over to inside of skirt; blindstitch in place. Insert elastic band and sew ends tog.

- Using crochet hook, finish hemline with 1 row of sc using 1 strand each of all 3 yarns held tog.

- Block and steam skirt to desired measurements.

- Attach waistband of ready-made half-slip to bottom inside edge of waistband.

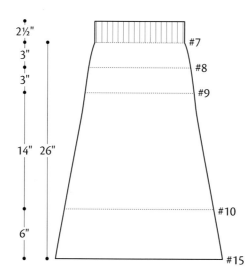

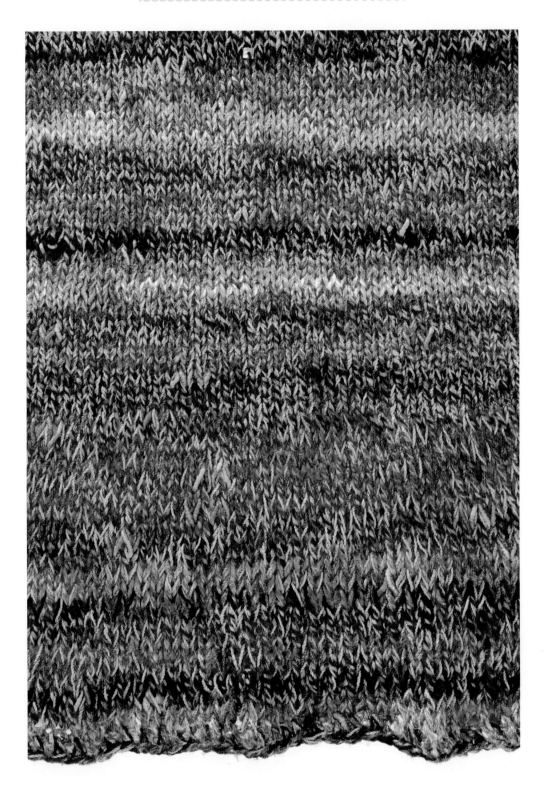

MADELINE

Lindy wanted the perfect basic ribbed skirt and this is it!
By varying both needle size and the width of the ribs as
she knit, Lindy was able to create the shaping required
and give the skirt visual interest as well.

SIZES

Extra Small
(Small, Medium, Large, Extra Large)

Actual Hip Measurement:
35 (36½, 38, 42, 47½)"

Finished Hip Measurement:
33 (34½, 36, 40, 45½)"

Finished Length: 30"*

*Finished length is measured from bottom of
waistband. Length of skirt can be altered as
desired by lengthening or shortening skirt
in section worked on size 6 needle.*

MATERIALS

8 (10, 10, 10, 12) skeins of Dream from Tahki, color 023 Chocolate Brown

US 7, 6, and 5 circular needles, all 24" to 26" long, or size to obtain gauge

Stitch marker

1"-wide nonrolling elastic cut to same length as actual waist measurement

Ready-made half-slip at least 3" shorter than finished length of skirt

GAUGE

A yarn or combination of yarns that, when held tog as one, knits to 24 sts over 4" in K3, P2 ribbing (steamed) on size 6 needle

DIRECTIONS

- With size 7 needle and 2 strands of Dream held tog, CO 250 (260, 270, 300, 340) sts and set up patt on next (WS) row: *P3, K2, rep from * across. Work back and forth in established ribbing for 3 more rows. Join into rnd, taking care not to twist sts; pm and cont in rnd, working K3, P2 ribbing.

- At 8" from bottom, switch to size 6 needle and cont in ribbing.

- At 20" from bottom, work dec as follows: *K3, P2, K3, P2tog, rep from *—225 (234, 243, 270, 306) sts. Cont in new (K3, P2, K3, P1) ribbing.

- At 24" from bottom, switch to size 5 needle and work next dec as follows: *K3, P2tog, K3, P1, rep from *—200 (208, 216, 240, 272) sts. Cont in new (K3, P1) ribbing.

- At 26" from bottom, work next dec as follows: *K3, K2tog, K2, P1, rep from *—175 (182, 189, 210, 238) sts. Cont in new (K6, P1) ribbing.

- At 30" from bottom, set up waistband ribbing as follows: *K1, P1, K2tog, P1, K1, P1, rep from *—150 (156, 162, 184, 204) sts. Cont in K1, P1 ribbing for 1½".

- BO all sts in patt.

FINISHING

- Finish waistband using Style C (see page 76).

- Block skirt and steam to desired measurement. Do not oversteam as it will be difficult to reduce the size if steamed too large.

- Attach waistband of ready-made half-slip to bottom inside edge of waistband.

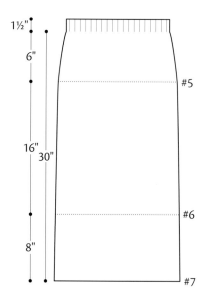

NAOMI

Missoni-style color work with its bold use of color and crisp, geometric lines has always been a favorite of ours. Beryl found the perfect multicolor space-dyed wool to create the body of the skirt and set off the color-work border patterns. This is definitely not a beginner's project—but well worth the effort.

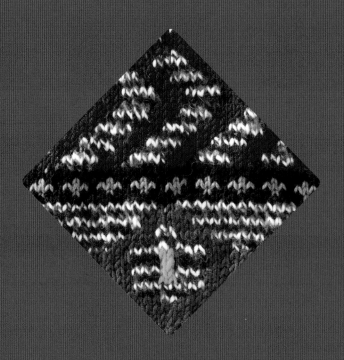

SIZES

Small
(Medium, Large)

Actual Hip Measurement:
34 (38, 42)"

Finished Hip Measurement:
32 (36, 40)"

Finished Length: 28"*

Finished length is measured from bottom of waistband. Length of skirt can be altered as desired by lengthening or shortening skirt in section worked on size 8 needle.

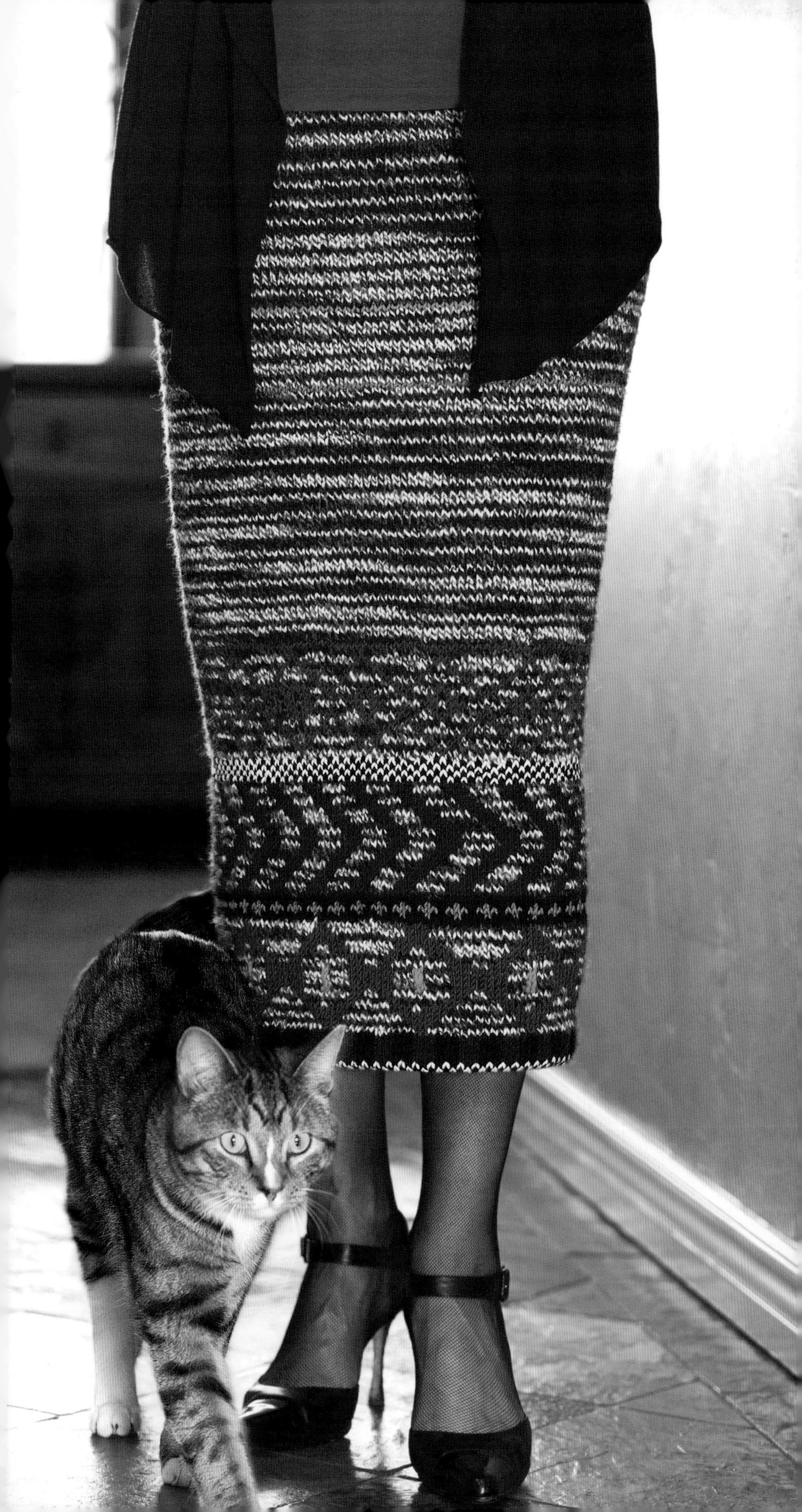

MATERIALS

A 6 (6, 7) skeins of Sempre from Filatura di Crosa, color 1 Black/White Multi

Zara from Filatura di Crosa in the following amounts and colors:

B 1 skein of color 1404 Black

C 1 skein of color 1396 White

D 1 skein of color 1523 Purple

E 1 skein of color 1490 Periwinkle

F 1 skein of color 1503 Bronze

G 1 skein of color 1461 Wine

H 1 skein of color 1745 Olive

I 1 skein of color 1734 Teal

US 8, 7, and 6 circular needles, all 24" to 26" long, or size to obtain gauge

8 stitch markers

1"-wide nonrolling elastic cut to same length as actual waist measurement

Ready-made half-slip at least 2" shorter than finished length of skirt

GAUGE

A yarn or combination of yarns that, when held tog as one, knits to 16 sts over 4" in St st on size 8 needle

DIRECTIONS

NOTE: *When working color-work portions of this skirt, it is important to remember that color work naturally pulls in a bit. (We found that our gauge changed from 4.0 to 4.4 sts per 1" when working with two colors. The numbers of stitches have been adjusted accordingly.) Do take care not to pull yarns too tightly when knitting in color work. The finished piece will steam open a bit.*

- With size 7 needle and B, CO 134 (134, 140) sts. Join into rnd, taking care not to twist sts; pm and knit every rnd for 1", inc 28 (28, 34) sts evenly spaced in last rnd—162 (162, 174) sts.

- **Work 3 rnds of color work:** K1 with B, K1 with C, offsetting colors on alternate rnds to create a checkerboard effect.

- **Work 5 rnds of color work:** K3 with B, K3 with D.

- **Next rnd:** With B, knit and dec 2 sts for Small and Medium sizes or inc 2 sts for Large in this rnd—160 (160, 176) sts.

- Work graph 1 with A, I, and E for 18 rnds.

- Work graph 2 with B and F for 5 rnds.

- Work graph 3 with A and G for 19 rnds.

- **Work 4 rnds of color work:** K1 in B, K1 in C, offsetting colors on alternate rnds to create a checkerboard effect.

- **Next rnd:** With A, knit and dec 4 sts (inc 8 sts, inc 4 sts) evenly spaced in rnd—156 (168, 180) sts.

- Work graph 4 with A and H for 17 rnds.

- **Next rnd:** Switch to size 8 needle and A, knit and dec 20 (12, 12) sts evenly spaced in this rnd—136 (156, 168) sts.

- Cont to knit every rnd, and at 2" intervals, work 1 rnd of each solid color in following order: D, E, F, G, H, I.

- At 23" from bottom, switch to size 7 needle and A, knit every rnd.

- At 26" from bottom, switch to size 6 needle and cont with A.

- At 29" from bottom, cont with A and work in K1, P1 ribbing for 2½".

- BO all sts in patt.

FINISHING

- Fold 1¼" of waistband over to inside of skirt; blindstitch in place. Insert elastic band and sew ends tog.

- Fold 1" of bottom hem to inside and blindstitch in place. Press lightly when steaming to set.

- Block and steam skirt to desired measurements.

- Attach waistband of ready-made half-slip to bottom inside edge of waistband.

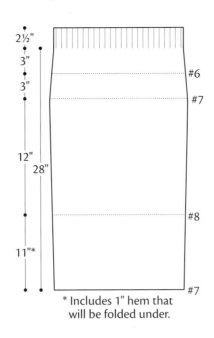

2½"
3"
3"
12"
28"
11"*

#6
#7
#8
#7

* Includes 1" hem that
will be folded under.

Graph 1
Multiple of 16 sts

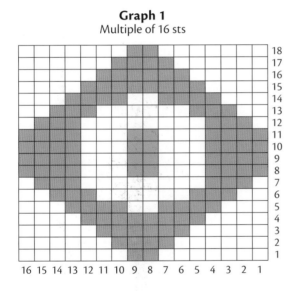

18
17
16
15
14
13
12
11
10
9
8
7
6
5
4
3
2
1

16 15 14 13 12 11 10 9 8 7 6 5 4 3 2 1

Graph 2
Multiple of 4 sts

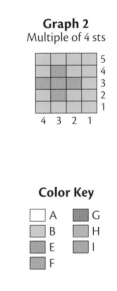

5
4
3
2
1

4 3 2 1

Color Key

A   G
B   H
E   I
F

Graph 3
Multiple of 8 sts

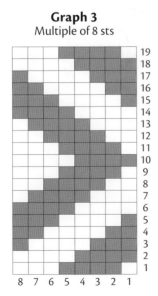

19
18
17
16
15
14
13
12
11
10
9
8
7
6
5
4
3
2
1

8 7 6 5 4 3 2 1

Graph 4
Multiple of 12 sts

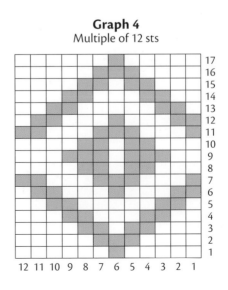

17
16
15
14
13
12
11
10
9
8
7
6
5
4
3
2
1

12 11 10 9 8 7 6 5 4 3 2 1

OLIVIA

Lindy had an idea of what she wanted this skirt to look
like but she truly wasn't certain it would work until it was all
completed! The body of the skirt is knit in panels, the stitches are
picked up and knit into the round at the hip, and the ribbing gives
it a low-waisted band that looks great with a variety of belts.

SIZES

Small
(Medium, Large, Extra Large)

Actual Hip Measurement:
35 (38, 41, 44)"

Finished Hip Measurement:
33 (36, 39, 42)"

Finished Length: 30"*

*Finished length is measured from bottom of
waistband. Length of skirt can be altered as
desired by lengthening or shortening skirt
in section worked on size 8 needle.*

MATERIALS

A   8 (9, 9, 10) skeins of 127 Print from
    Filatura di Crosa, color 18 Black Multi

B   3 (4, 4, 4) skeins of Dream from Tahki,
    color 015 Black

C   2 (2, 2, 3) skeins of Suede from Berroco,
    color 3729 Zorro

Size 8 straight or circular needles or size to
    obtain gauge

Size 6 circular needle, 24" to 26" long

6 stitch holders

Size H-8 (5 mm) crochet hook

1 card of elastic thread in color to match
    yarn

Ready-made half-slip at least 3" shorter than
    finished length of skirt

GAUGE

A yarn or combination of yarns that, when
held tog as one, knits to 16 sts and 20 rows
over 4" in St st on size 8 needles

DIRECTIONS

Make 6 panels.

*   With size 8 needles and 1 strand each
    of A and B held tog, CO 36 (38, 40, 42)
    sts and work 4 rows in K2, P2 ribbing.

*   Working in St st, dec 1 st at each end
    every 18 rows (approx 3") 6 times—24
    (26, 28, 30) sts.

*   Cont in St st until panel measures 22"
    from bottom, place sts on a holder.

FINISHING

*   With RS tog, sew 6 panels tog from WS
    so that seams are exposed on RS.

*   Using crochet hook, and 2 strands of C
    held tog, sc over all exposed seams from
    top to bottom.

*   Using crochet hook, and size 6 needle
    and 1 strand each of A and B held
    tog, PU 144 (156, 168,180) sts from
    st holders. On next row, set up K2,
    P2 ribbing patt as you K2tog *on each
    side* of the 6 seams where panels are
    joined—132 (144, 156, 168) sts. Cont in
    ribbing patt in the rnd for approx 8".

*   At 30" from bottom, BO all sts loosely.

*   Run 2 strands of elastic held tog along
    inside of ribbing at 1" intervals 3 times
    for a more secure fit.

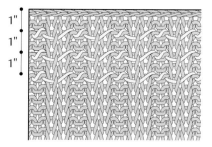

*   Block and steam skirt to desired
    measurements.

*   Attach waistband of ready-made half-
    slip to bottom inside edge of waistband.

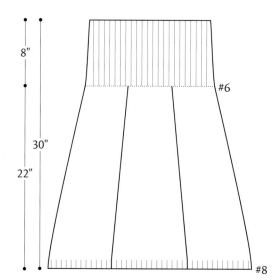

PALOMA

This skirt actually evolved as it was knit. Beryl realized several inches into it that she found the "wrong" side of the work much more textural and interesting than the right side. We realized about halfway up that the ends of each yarn cut as Beryl changed yarns created a very interesting fringe! This is a lesson in keeping your mind open to new ideas as you knit.

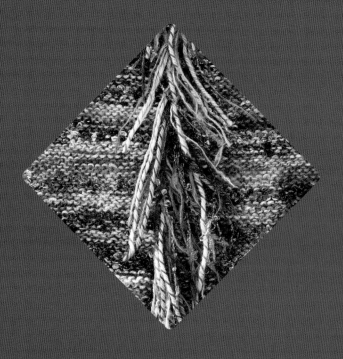

SIZES

Extra Small
(Small, Medium, Large, Extra Large)

Actual Hip Measurement:
34 (36, 38, 40, 42)"

Finished Hip Measurement:
32 (34, 36, 38, 40)"

Finished Length: 27"*

Finished length is measured from bottom of waistband. Length of skirt can be altered as desired by lengthening or shortening skirt in section worked on size 8 needle.

MATERIALS

A   1 skein of Geisha from Blue Moon Fiber Arts, color Carbon

B   1 skein of Lupe from Blue Moon Fiber Arts, color Carbon

C   1 skein of Silk Mo from Blue Moon Fiber Arts, color Carbon

D   1 skein of Twisted! from Blue Moon Fiber Arts, color Carbon

US 8, 7, and 6 circular needles, all 24" to 26" long, or size to obtain gauge

Stitch marker

1"-wide nonrolling elastic cut to same length as actual waist measurement

Ready-made half-slip at least 3" shorter than finished length of skirt

GAUGE

A yarn or combination of yarns that, when held tog as one, knits to 17.25 sts over 4" in St st on size 8 needles

STRIPING PATTERN

2 rows with 1 strand each of A and B held tog

2 rows with 1 strand of D

2 rows with 1 strand each of A and C held tog

Rep 6 rows for striping patt, leaving approx 5" tails on each yarn every time you change yarns. This creates the vertical fringe on skirt.

DIRECTIONS

• With size 8 needle and 1 strand each of A and B held tog, CO 138 (148, 156, 164, 174) sts; join into rnd, taking care not to twist sts; pm and knit every rnd, working in striping patt.

• At 22" from bottom, switch to size 7 needle and knit every rnd for 3".

• At 25" from bottom, switch to size 6 needle and knit every rnd for 2".

• At 27" from bottom, switch to 1 strand of D and work in K1, P1 ribbing for 2½".

• BO all sts in patt.

FINISHING

• Fold 1¼" of waistband over to inside of skirt; blindstitch in place. Insert elastic band and sew ends tog.

• Trim fringe evenly to 3" lengths.

• Block and steam skirt to desired measurements.

• Attach waistband of ready-made half-slip to bottom inside edge of waistband.

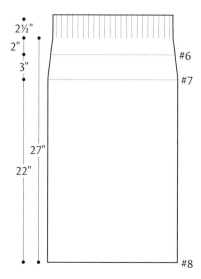

ABBREVIATIONS AND GLOSSARY

approx	approximately	**patt**	pattern
beg	begin(ning)	**pm**	place marker
BO	bind off	**PU**	pick up and knit
CO	cast on	**pw**	purlwise
CC	contrasting color	**rem**	remain(ing)
cont	continue, continuing	**rep**	repeat
dec	decrease, decreasing	**RS**	right side
EOR	every other row	**sc**	single crochet
garter st	garter stitch (in the round: knit 1 round, purl 1 round)	**sl**	slip as if to purl unless otherwise noted
inc	increase, increasing	**st(s)**	stitch(es)
K	knit	**St st**	stockinette stitch (in the round: knit every round; back and forth: knit on right side, purl on wrong side)
K1tbl	knit one stitch through the back loop		
K2tog	knit two stitches together as one (one-stitch decrease)	**tog**	together
MC	main color	**WS**	wrong side
oz	ounces	**wyif**	with yarn in front
P	purl	**YO**	yarn over
P2tog	purl two stitches together as one (one-stitch decrease)		

SPECIAL TECHNIQUES

Below are instructions for the special stitches used in the skirts in this book.

THE CHINESE CAST ON (FOR FELICITY SKIRT)

This cast on provides a nonrolling edge. This is a technique for intermediate and experienced knitters. For less-experienced knitters, use a standard cast on and then finish the hem of the skirt with a crochet edge. The technique consists of the cast on plus rows 1 and 2.

Cast on: Hold the tail and working yarn with your left hand as for the long-tail cast on. Do not make a slipknot on the right-hand needle.

1. With the yarn sitting on top of the right-hand needle (no slipknot), hold this loop with your right index finger, then take the right-hand needle around the back and under the yarn on your index finger, then toward you, under and over the yarn on your thumb, and then back under the yarn on the index finger. This puts one stitch on the right-hand needle.

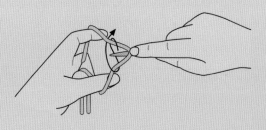

2. For the next stitch, move the right-hand needle toward you, over and under the yarn on your thumb, then over and around the back of the yarn on your index finger, and back under the yarn on your thumb. This puts another stitch on the needle.

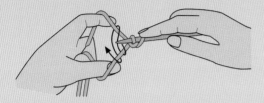

Repeat steps 1 and 2 until you have the required number of stitches cast on to the needle.

Work the next 2 rows as follows:

Row 1: K1 (edge st), *sl 1 wyif pw, K1tbl, rep from * to last st, K1 (edge st).

Row 2: K1 (edge st), *sl 1 wyif pw, K1, rep from * to last st, K1 (edge st).

On the next row, begin the pattern as indicated in the directions.

TWISTED CORD (FOR KATERINA SKIRT)

Cut 1 strand of A four times longer than the finished length. Fold strand in half and knot the ends. Loop one end over a hook, and insert a knitting needle into the other end. Turn the needle around and around until the strands are twisted enough so that when you relax the cord, it twists into tight knots. Keeping the cord taut, fold it in half and let the cord twist onto itself. Tie the ends.

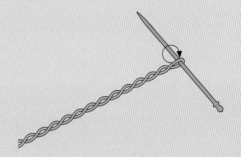

WAISTBAND OPTIONS

We have found that personal preference plays an important part in finishing the waistband of skirts, so we have included several of the methods we found that work well. Most of the skirts in this book can be finished with any of the methods detailed below. In the patterns where a different type of skirt finishing is required, we have noted it in that pattern.

STYLE A (STANDARD WAISTBAND)

- With needle one size smaller than last size used on body of skirt, using same yarn(s), work in K1, P1 ribbing for 2½" or length indicated in directions. Bind off all stitches loosely in pattern in same-size needle on which ribbing was knit.

- Fold waistband over in half to inside of skirt, blindstitch in place, and insert elastic band. Sew ends to secure.

STYLE B (LIGHTER-WEIGHT VERSION OF STYLE A)

- With needle two or three sizes smaller than last size used on body of skirt, using only one of yarns from the body of the skirt (use the most durable/stable of the fibers), work in K1, P1 ribbing for 2½" or length indicated in directions. Bind off all stitches loosely in pattern on a needle two sizes larger than that on which ribbing was knit.

- Fold waistband over in half to inside of skirt, blindstitch in place, and insert elastic band. Sew ends to secure.

Style C (Alternate Flat Waistband)

- With needle one size smaller than last size used on body of skirt, using same yarn(s), work in K1, P1 ribbing for 1¼" or length indicated in directions. Bind off all stitches loosely in pattern on same-size needle on which ribbing was knit.

- With same yarn(s) used for waistband threaded on a tapestry needle and working on the inside of the waistband, create a pattern of Vs and upside-down Vs as shown below.

- Insert elastic band into the framework you have just created, and sew the ends to secure.

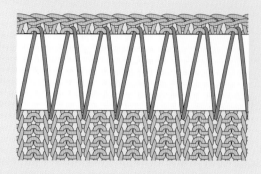

TRICOTER SERVICES

We offer complimentary design services and guidance through the completion of projects to all of our customers. We believe that it is the detail and finishing that elevates a garment from "loving-hands-at-home" to a beautiful handknit original. We offer a variety of classes from basic skills through advanced techniques and finishing.

We are happy to help in the selection of appropriate fibers for any project you may have chosen should you need or desire assistance. Any of the sweaters or projects in our books can be "kitted" to your specifications. Please don't hesitate to contact us.

Expert Finishing

Because we realize your time is precious and limited, Tricoter is also pleased to offer a variety of custom knitting and finishing services for those occasions when you require professional assistance. We have a number of out-of-town customers with whom we work on a regular basis to assist in the completion of hand-knit garments. Finishing services are available for the detailing of your completed pieces. Please contact us for an estimate for these services.

Custom Hand Knitting

We offer a variety of custom knitting services for your convenience. All garments are individually fitted and beautifully finished. We will work with you to design and create a sweater, jacket, coat, or garment of your choice reflecting your individual style. (We can knit any of the sweaters in this book for you.) Estimates available upon request.

Please feel free to contact us by calling (206) 328-6505 or by emailing us at tricoter@tricoter.com for additional information regarding any of these services.

YARN INFORMATION

Yarn-Weight Symbols						
Yarn Weight Symbol and Category Names	**1** Super fine	**2** Fine	**3** Light	**4** Medium	**5** Bulky	**6** Super bulky
Type of Yarns in Category	Sock, Fingering, Baby	Sport, Baby	DK, Light Worsted	Worsted, Afghan, Aran	Chunky, Craft, Rug	Bulky, Roving
Knit Gauge Ranges in Stockinette Stitch to 4"	27 to 32 sts	23 to 26 sts	21 to 24 sts	16 to 20 sts	12 to 15 sts	6 to 11 sts
Recommended Needle in U.S. Size Range	1 to 3	3 to 5	5 to 7	7 to 9	9 to 11	11 and larger

METRIC CONVERSIONS

$$m = yds \times 0.9144$$

$$yds = m \times 1.0936$$

$$g = oz \times 28.35$$

$$oz = g \times 0.0352$$

YARNS

Baby Cashmerino 3
Debbie Bliss Inc./KFI Inc.
55% merino,
   33% microfibre,
   12% cashmere
137 yards

Baby Kid Extra 2
Filatura di Crosa/TSC Inc.
80% super kid mohair,
   20% nylon
268 yards

Big Wool Fusion 6
Rowan/Westminster
   Fibers Inc.
100% wool
87 yards

Boise 5
Karabella
50% cashmere, 50%
   superfine merino wool
163 yards

Cashmere 100 4
Filatura di Crosa/TSC Inc.
100% cashmere
154 yards

Cashmere 7000 2
Filatura di Crosa/TSC Inc.
100% cashmere
385 yards

Cashmerino Astrakhan 4
Debbie Bliss Inc./KFI Inc.
60% wool,
   30% microfibre,
   10% cashmere
83 yards

Cleo 4
Muench Yarns Inc.
87% viscose, 13% metal
62 yards

Cork Chenille 4
Habu Textiles
100% cotton
99 yards

Diacosta 3
Diakeito/Dancing Fibers Inc.
53% acrylic, 47% viscose
149 yards

Dialent 2
Diakeito/Dancing Fibers Inc.
40% acrylic, 24% viscose, 18% ramie, 11% cotton, 6% polyester, 1% nylon
150 yards

Diasantafe 2
Diakeito/Dancing Fibers Inc.
50% viscose, 34% raime, 16% nylon
140 yards

Dream 2
Dream Print 2
Tahki Yarns/TSC Inc.
80% wool, 20% nylon
262 yards

Geisha 3
Blue Moon Fiber Arts
64% kid mohair, 20% mulberry silk, 16% nylon
495 yards

Gioiello 2
Filatura di Crosa/TSC Inc.
30% kid mohair, 30% extra fine merino wool, 20% nylon, 10% cotton, 10% acrylic
220 yards

Glowlash 5
Erdal Yarns Ltd.
85% rayon, 15% Lurex
104 yards

Kidsilk Night 1
Rowan/Westminster Fibers Inc.
67% super kid mohair, 18% silk, 10% polyester, 5% nylon
227 yards

Lazer FX 1
Berroco Inc.
100% polyester
70 yards

Lupe 3
Blue Moon Fiber Arts
100% nylon bouclé
300 yards

Opal Lamé 3
Berroco Inc./Lang Yarns
77% viscose, 15% nylon, 8% polyester
137 yards

Poly Moire Eyelash 2
Habu Textiles
100% polyester
23 yards

127 Print 4
Filatura di Crosa/TSC Inc.
100% wool
92 yards

Rayon Metallic 2
Blue Heron Yarns
85% rayon, 15% metal
550 yards

Sakura 3
Noro/KFI Inc.
36% rayon, 28% polyester, 18% nylon, 11% silk, 7% lamb's wool
146 yards

Sempre 5
Filatura di Crosa/TSC Inc.
95% wool, 5% polymid
105 yards

Shingle 2
Louisa Harding/Euro Yarns Inc.
90% polyester, 10% pailettes
87 yards

Silk/Cashmere 2
Jade Sapphire Exotic Fibres
55% silk, 45% Mongolian cashmere
400 yards

Silk Mo 2
Blue Moon Fiber Arts
64% kid mohair, 20% mulberry silk, 16% nylon
794 yards

Socks that Rock 3
Blue Moon Fiber Arts
100% superwash merino—lightweight
360 yards

Soft Kid 2
GGH/Muench Yarns
70% super kid mohair, 25% nylon, 5% wool
151 yards

Stained Glass 2
Ironstone Yarns
100% rayon
200 yards

Suede 4
Berroco Inc.
100% nylon
120 yards

Tobi Moire 2
Habu Textiles Inc.
100% polyester
137 yards

Twisted! 4
Blue Moon Fiber Arts
100% merino wool
560 yards

Victoria 4
S. Charles Collezione / TSC Inc
60% cotton, 40% viscose
70 yards

Wool Cotton 3
Rowan Yarns
50% merino wool, 50% cotton
123 yards

Zara 5
Filatura di Crosa/TSC Inc.
100% merino wool
137 yards

RESOURCE LIST

For a list of shops in your area that carry
the yarns mentioned in this book, contact
the following companies.

Berroco Inc.
www.berroco.com

Blue Heron Yarns
www.blueheronyarns.com

Blue Moon Fiber Arts
www.bluemoonfiberarts.com

Dancing Fibers
www.dancingfibers.com

Erdal Yarns
www.erdal.com

Habu Textiles
www.habutextiles.com

Ironstone Yarns
PO Box 8
Las Vegas, NM 87701-0008
(800)-343-4914

Jade Sapphire
www.jadesapphire.com

Karabella Yarns Inc.
www.karabellayarns.com

Knitting Fever Inc.
www.knittingfever.com

Muench Yarns Inc.
www.muenchyarns.com

**Tahki, S. Charles Collezione,
and Filatura di Crosa**
www.tahkistacycharles.com

Westminster Fibers Inc.
4 Townsend West, Unit B
Nashua, NH 03063
(800) 433-7899

ABOUT THE AUTHORS

Beryl and Linden joined forces in 1993 and became partners in their shop Tricoter the following year. Beryl's lifelong passion for and knowledge of knitting, and Linden's retail design background and love of color and texture have proven successful for the team.

Beryl, born and raised in Vancouver, B.C., grew up in knitting shops where her mother, after purchasing beautiful fibers for her daughter, would drop her off to spend Saturdays knitting with shop owners and customers. An avid gardener, cook, and entertainer, Beryl has also found success as hostess and teacher at Tricoter.

Linden, raised in Southern California, moved to Seattle from New York City in the 1990s to transition from an 18-year career in visual merchandising and design with May Department Stores and Liz Claiborne. Initially believing she wanted to escape retail, Linden became a partner in a start-up coffee company, but after a chance meeting with Beryl, she realized that destiny had another plan.

A partnership was forged within a year, and the two women remain close friends as well as business partners and coauthors. They even lived together for seven years, until one got married and the other became engaged.

"Our plan is to grow old together knitting here at Tricoter a few days a week," says Beryl. "We'll probably have to speak a little louder and move a little slower, but there isn't any place we'd rather be, or anything we'd rather be doing!"